A BOOK FOR MOM — MUSIC FOR BABY

Lullabies & Daydreams

Compiled by Lois L. Kaufman
Original text by Suzanne Siegel Zenkel

Illustrated by Amy Dietrich

Designed by Arlene Greco

Peter Pauper Press, Inc.
WHITE PLAINS, NEW YORK

Copyright © 1997
Peter Pauper Press, Inc.
202 Mamaroneck Avenue
White Plains, NY 10601
All rights reserved
ISBN 0-88088-411-8
Printed in China
7 6 5 4 3 2 1

Contents

Falling in Love With Your Baby

Have Confidence in Your Instincts

Time for Yourself

A Question of Balance

A Newfound Appreciation for Our Own Mothers

New Friendships

Savor Each Moment

Falling in Love With Your Baby

Having a baby is like falling in love. Suddenly life is infused with the sweet joy of discovery, and the ordinary seems unimaginably extraordinary. From the beginning, your baby presents you with an unending stream of new and special things to behold. As you delight in the wonder of each new expression and personality trait, hours pass unnoticed. You have spent them gazing in awe at your miracle, your baby.

Remarkably, your feelings about your baby are reciprocated from the very first moment. Nowhere is love more mutual, complete, and immediate than in the bond between mother and infant. Your baby responds to your love with outstretched arms. Its attachment to you is stronger than the grip of its tiny fist wrapped around your finger.

There is no better lesson than parenting to teach us once again how to give and receive love. Having a child is the most natural means of experiencing love in its most pure, potent, and unwavering form. Greatest of all, it will grow deeper and stronger with each passing day. The best is yet to come!

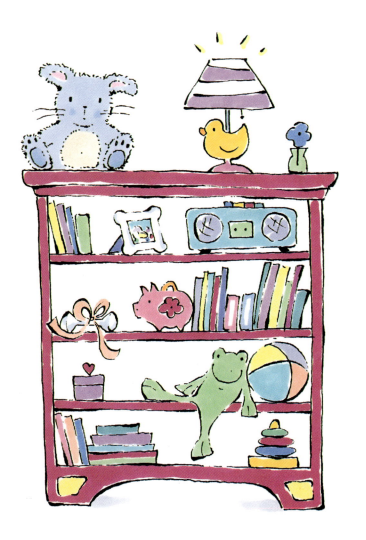

We're more thrilled than we ever imagined! Somehow I never actually thought this would happen to me. It may sound funny, but I'm so happy with myself. It's as if I am the first person ever to be pregnant! I can't think of an act that's more creative or more fulfilling.

Anonymous

I am . . . looking forward to the wonder-filled, miraculous moment when my husband and I greet our child for the first time. It is the most joyous time . . . there is no way to fully define or explain it.

Irene Bubnack

How beautifully everything is arranged by Nature; as soon as a child enters the world, it finds a mother ready to take care of it.
Jules Michelet

I stood in the hospital corridor the night after she was born. Through a window I could see all the small, crying newborn infants and somewhere among them slept the one who was mine. I stood there for hours filled with happiness until the night nurse sent me to bed.
Liv Ullmann

Sleep, baby, sleep!
Thy father's watching the sheep,
Thy mother's shaking the dreamland tree,
And down drops a little dream for thee.
Sleep, baby, sleep.
Elizabeth Prentiss

The babe at first feeds upon the mother's
bosom, but is always on her heart.
Henry Ward Beecher

The sweetest flowers in all the world—
A baby's hands.
Algernon Charles Swinburne

Children are life renewing itself, Captain Butler. And when life does that, danger seems very unimportant.
Spoken by Olivia de Havilland,
Gone with the Wind

She's more fun to watch than an ant farm.
John Goodman,
about his daughter

The world has no flower in any land,
And no such pearl in any gulf or sea,
As any babe on any mother's knee.
Algernon Charles Swinburne

Where yet was ever found the mother,
who'd change her booby for another?

John Gay

Here we have a baby. It is composed of a bald head and a pair of lungs.

Eugene Field

The worst feature of a new baby is its mother's singing.

Kin Hubbard

Cherishing children is the mark of a civilized society.

Joan Ganz Cooney

Have Confidence in Your Instincts

Have confidence in your instincts; they will serve you well. Though today's new mother may have achieved feats of monumental proportions in school or at work, she still ventures into motherhood as a wobbly-legged beginner. Even the most confident among us have moments of doubt and confusion. The actress Tammy Grimes, mother of actress Amanda Plummer, once said, *We can't compare ourselves to the unattainable perfection of imaginary parents.* We can only hold ourselves up to the high standards that we, as intelligent and caring women, set for ourselves. In these enlightened times, we are offered the well-meaning "how tos" of parenting from every angle—the media, our friends, our family.

It pays to recognize that there's no set formula for success, and that so often the answers lie within you and your baby. When in doubt, look to your past and consider how well your intuition has served you. Then apply your sound judgment to the issue at hand, and move on. Your confidence in your parenting skills will increase tenfold with each decision made and each problem solved. Don't be afraid to take a stand and try a new approach. Do what works for you and your baby. Recognize your special qualities as a mother and have faith. Your self-assurance will not only stand *you* in good stead, it will also help you set an example for your child, enabling him or her to become a confident and independent person.

Parents have become so convinced that educators know what is best for children that they forget that they themselves are really the experts.
Marian Wright Edelman

I knew having a baby would teach me about deep feelings of love, but I didn't know it would teach me so much about sharing.
Deidre Hall

Although today there are many trial marriages, there is no such thing as a trial child.
Gail Sheehy

Children in a family are like flowers in a bouquet: there's always one determined to face in an opposite direction from the way the arranger desires.
Marcelene Cox

Don't be afraid to kiss your baby when you feel like it.
Dr. Benjamin Spock

Spock, shlock, don't talk to me about that stuff. A man doesn't know how to bring up children until he's been a mother.
Dan Greenburg

Children don't have to be raised. They'll grow.
>> *Buffy Sainte-Marie*

You were once a new baby. You had a special place in your family then—and you still have a special place in your family now. You always will—no matter how many children your mom and dad have.
>> *Mr. Rogers*

If you want a baby, have a new one. Don't baby the old one.
>> *Jessamyn West*

The main purpose of children's parties is to remind you that there are children more awful than your own.
        Katharine Whitehorn

Babies are such a nice way to start people.
        Don Herold

If you bungle raising your children, I don't think whatever else you do well matters very much.
        Jacqueline Onassis

If you can laugh at something later, you might as well laugh at the time.
        Marie Osmond

Time for Yourself

Those wondrous first weeks between mother and child are filled with tender moments, yet it is only natural for Mommy to need a few tender moments to herself! With the flurry of new activity in your life, it is not easy to believe that there are still 24 hours in a day. Remember that those hours still exist and make sure at least one of them belongs to you! As accomplished hardworking women, we're used to achieving great feats of endurance, and there's nothing like motherhood to put you to the test. Seize the day—don't let it seize you! Use the time when your baby naps to relax. From time to time, reward yourself by accepting the offer of a friend or family member to watch the baby. A quiet moment of solitude and tranquility can do wonders for you. It's also good for your baby to know and appreciate loved ones. Enjoy some personal time, whether you spend it with your husband, a treasured friend, or curled up with a good book. The rays of joy and contentment radiate from generation to generation. Remember that in taking care of yourself, you are taking better care of your baby.

We are all born rude. No infant has ever appeared yet with the grace to understand how inconsiderate it is to disturb others in the middle of the night.
Judith Martin

The ideal thing, the perfect solution, would be to have sextuplets when you were in your early twenties. Then, when the children were two years old, *all* of them would untie their shoelaces and remove their shoes. It would be quite a pile of shoes, but once that phase was over it would be over.
Jean Kerr

When my children become unruly, I use a playpen. When they're finished, I climb out.
Erma Bombeck

There is no such thing as a non-working mother.
Hester Mundis

Remember that in taking care of yourself, you are taking better care of your baby. The art of being a parent is to sleep when the baby isn't looking.
Anonymous

Have children while your parents are still young enough to take care of them.
Rita Rudner

One grandmother will spoil a baby. Two working together will bring him up in the way he should go, for each will suspect the other of spoiling him and will check it.
William Allen White

Babies don't come with directions on the back or batteries that can be removed. Motherhood is twenty-four hours a day, seven days a week. You can't "leave the office."
Pat Schroeder

Everything is scheduled. Fifteen minutes has become a substantial period of time. If I brush my hair once, if I read to my children, then that's a good day.

Jacquelyn Mitchard

Sometimes I feel overwhelmed. But I don't think you would find any mother of 8-month-olds who wouldn't say that.

Patty Shier,
mother of quintuplets

One of the greatest labor-saving inventions of today is tomorrow.

Vincent T. Foss

A Question of Balance

Like a richly textured work of art in progress, your new life with baby is a kaleidoscope of beautiful, ever-changing experiences.

One of the most constructive tasks for a new mother to undertake is to master the great balancing act that parenthood necessitates. In the first few months, being a mother may feel surprisingly comfortable and natural, but everything else may feel a little bit awkward. The good news is that these awkward feelings are temporary. While it may feel confusing, the challenge is simple: prioritize the tasks before you, giving greater weight to those things that bring you the most fulfillment. With each passing day, you will be better equipped to combine motherhood with your other work and interests. The new demands a baby imposes on your time and energy compel you to use your free time very wisely. Once you've gained a sense of equilibrium, you may well find that you've embarked on a period of intense productivity. You may even have a newfound appreciation for your own resourcefulness.

A newborn baby has the uncanny ability to help you streamline and refine your interests, more clearly set your everyday goals, and see your future dreams more vividly. Rest assured that the various facets of your life can complement rather than conflict with one another. Soon your timetable will adjust and the joy and fulfillment of motherhood will grow.

At work, you think of the children you've left at home. At home, you think of the work you've left unfinished. Such a struggle is unleashed within yourself: your heart is rent.
Golda Meir

We don't know how resourceful we are until we have a child. It is such a basic instinct to accommodate a child into one's life.
Tina Brown

I think that people have children once they've arrived and they feel they have something to offer. Maybe it's also saying that their fame, their success, hasn't given them true fulfillment.
Dr. Don Lombardi

Another thing that seems quite helpful to the creative process is having babies. It does not detract at all from one's creativity. It reminds one that there is always more where that came from and there is never any shortage of ideas or of the ability to create.
Fay Weldon

Now, basically, if they want you to do a job, you say, "Well, my baby comes with me." What are they going to say—no?
Gigi Rice

A father finds out what is meant by "a spitting image" when he tries to feed cereal to an infant.
Imogene Fey

It's very difficult to be married and write, to be unmarried and write, to have children or not have children and write.
Laurel Speer

I think we both knew we wanted a baby and wanted one with each other. That's the thing about falling in love with a friend. You know what kind of father he'll be. Both my sons are very lucky.
Nana Visitor

I have Lisa. That's better than any gold medal.
Zola Budd Pieterse

A Newfound Appreciation for Our Own Mothers

There's nothing quite like motherhood itself to make you appreciate your own mother! The business of parenting is phenomenally demanding, with an astounding job description calling for talents and characteristics of mythic proportions. From her never-ending stream of small kindnesses to her grand heroic sacrifices, a mother pours her heart and soul into her children. Often at breakneck pace, yet almost always with the patience of a saint, a mother juggles commitments from many different directions.

Somehow she manages to keep all the balls aloft with grace and equanimity.

Once we ourselves are blessed to become mothers, we understand how natural it is to put our child's needs before our own. We also recognize the many precious gifts our own mothers bestowed upon us—riches we may once have taken for granted. We hear our mother's voice echo in our own and are pleasantly surprised by the familiar tones. Experience is indeed a wonderful teacher, and we should consider ourselves supremely lucky if we are able to learn from that of our own mothers.

God knows that a mother needs fortitude and courage and tolerance and flexibility and patience and firmness and nearly every other brave aspect of the human soul. But because I happen to be a parent of almost fiercely maternal nature, I praise *casualness*. It seems to me that rarest of virtues. It is useful enough when children are small. It is important to the point of necessity when they are adolescents.

Phyllis McGinley

The best way to make children good is to make them happy.

Oscar Wilde

Babies are necessary to grown-ups. A new baby is like the beginning of all things—wonder, hope, a dream of possibilities. In a world that is cutting down its trees to build highways, losing its earth to concrete . . . babies are almost the only remaining link with nature, with the natural world of living things from which we spring.

Eda J. LeShan

Let me not forget that I am the daughter of a woman who bent her head, trembling, between the blades of a cactus, her wrinkled face full of ecstasy over the promise of a flower, a woman who herself never ceased to flower, untiringly, during three quarters of a century.

Colette

Making the decision to have a child—it's momentous. It is to decide forever to have your heart go walking around outside your body.

Elizabeth Stone

A mother's love is indeed the golden link that binds youth to age; and he is still but a child, however time may have furrowed his cheek, or silvered his brow, who can yet recall, with a softened heart, the fond devotion, or the gentle chidings, of the best friend that God ever gives us.

Christian Nestell Bovee

Babies on television never spit up on the Ultrasuede.
> *Erma Bombeck*

Shayla is [the best part of my life today], and my family life.... We plan to bring her up with good morals and good values. She is the shining star of my life right now.
> *Mary Lou Retton*

My love of the stage is like my love for my mother: a love that grows with age ...
> *Bai Fengxi*

A baby really changes you. Everything I thought was so important before is really just silliness.
Deidre Hall

The most wonderful sound our ears can hear is the sound of a new-born baby.
Anonymous

Some are kissing mothers and some are scolding mothers, but it is love just the same, and most mothers kiss and scold together.
Pearl S. Buck

My mother told me stories all the time . . . And in all of those stories she told me who I was, who I was supposed to be, whom I came from, and who would follow me. In this way, she taught me the meaning of the words she said, that all life is a circle and everything has a place within it. That's what she said and what she showed me in the things she did and the way she lives.

Paula Gunn Allen

One never notices what has been done; one can only see what remains to be done.

Marie Curie

Just as you inherit your mother's brown eyes, you inherit part of yourself.

Alice Walker

In spite of a childhood marked by more discipline than love—and in spite of the difficulty she and all parents find in giving their children something they themselves did not experience—my mother did her best to make us feel unique and worthwhile. Over and over again, in every way she knew how, she told us that we didn't need to earn her love. We were loved and valued (and therefore were lovable and valuable) *exactly as we were.*

Gloria Steinem

New Friendships

One of the nicest byproducts of motherhood is the easy emergence of new friendships between women. The experience of having a baby provides an instant common interest, linking one mother to another and often paving the way to lasting friendship. From park benches in cities to playgrounds in the country, mothers come together to share their experiences and exchange ideas and feelings. Since motherhood is so universal, the pool of potential friends is large and chances are you'll find a number of women with whom you'll connect. Try to link up with other mothers who share not only your interest in parenting, but other concerns as well. Seek out people who share your enthusiasm for the same hobbies and pastimes. These are the friendships that will flourish over time, for their roots run deeper and spread farther. You will find, too, that these are the women who will best understand your occasional moments of frustration or fatigue because they will experience them as well. Talk about diapers and sleeping habits will eventually give way to discourse on more global matters. As your children grow and become more multidimensional, so, too, will these special relationships.

Childbirth of course is not the grand finale but one point, albeit a very dramatic one, in the process of becoming a mother.
Sheila Kitzinger

First of all things, for friendship, there must be that delightful, indefinable state called feeling at ease with your companion,— . . . the one woman out of a multitude who interests you, who meets your thoughts and tastes.
Julia Duhring

The place where two friends first met is sacred to them all through their friendship, all the more sacred as their friendship deepens and grows old.
Phillips Brooks

We are all held in place by the pressure of the crowd around us. We must all lean upon others. Let us see that we lean gracefully and freely and acknowledge their support.
Margaret Collier Graham

Happiness quite unshared can scarcely be called happiness; it has no taste.
Charlotte Brontë

I like to help women help themselves, as that is, in my opinion, the best way to settle the woman question. Whatever we can do and do well we have a right to, and I don't think any one will deny us.
Louisa May Alcott

Today wherever women gather together it is not necessarily nurturing. It is coalition building. And if you feel the strain, you may be doing some good work.

Bernice Johnson Reagon

Friendship of a kind that cannot easily be reversed tomorrow must have its roots in common interests and shared beliefs, and even between nations, in some personal feeling.

Barbara Tuchman

As women we have a special connectedness with each other. . . . Other women share my experiences. Healing and connectedness are the same.

Anne Wilson Schaef

Savor Each Moment

Savor each and every moment. Though the days may sometimes seem endless, the years go by in a flash. Rediscover the universe through the eyes of your child. Experience the wonder and delight he or she feels about all the things in life that typically go unnoticed by the adult eye. If you remain conscious of the passage of time and treasure each day, the mundane and bland can seem incredibly exciting and rich. Concentrate on the special moments that you can devote entirely to your child, remembering to live each of them to the fullest. As your baby nestles snugly in your arms, breathe in that singularly sweet scent and allow yourself a sigh of contentment. In the twinkle of a sleepy eye, your baby will be grown up. Waste no time. Relax and enjoy the adventure!

It's an interesting fact that babies who won't smile for love or money will smile for vegetables. And the messier the vegetable the more they will smile. A baby with a mouth full of strained spinach is almost guaranteed to smile from ear to ear, while green rivulets ooze down into his neck and all over his wrapper.
Jean Kerr

We find delight in the beauty and happiness of children that makes the heart too big for the body.
Ralph Waldo Emerson

A baby is God's opinion that the world should go on.
Carl Sandburg

[In a big family] the first child is kind of like the first pancake. If it's not perfect, that's okay, there are a lot more coming along.

Antonin Scalia

A newborn baby is merely a small, noisy object, slightly fuzzy on one end, with no distinguishing marks to speak of except a mouth, and in color either a salmon pink or a deep sorrel, depending on whether it is going to grow up a blonde or a brunette. But to its immediate family it is without question the most phenomenal, the most astonishing, the most absolutely unparalleled thing that has yet occurred in the entire history of this planet.

Irvin S. Cobb

I feel great these days, though a little sleep-deprived. I witnessed the fragility of life, how everything hangs in a delicate balance. This baby has been through such a journey, and I am so proud of him.
*Melissa Gilbert,
about her son Michael, born prematurely*

Who can foretell for what high cause this darling of the gods was born?
Andrew Marvell

Children are likely to live up to what you believe of them.
Lady Bird Johnson

Beforehand I was much more of a pessimist about my life and maybe my longevity. . . . Since having my son, I don't think that anymore. I think I'm going to live to see him grow up. It's like you grow another heart, like someone kicks down a door that was sealed shut, and then the whole world—sunshine, flowers—falls through. I have such joy that I didn't think was possible.
Rosie O'Donnell

It is not possible for civilization to flow backwards while there is youth in the world.
Helen Keller